BRAVE

DOESN'T MEAN

YOU'RE NOT

SCARED.

IT MEANS

YOU GO ON

EVEN THOUGH YOU'RE

SCARED.

INTRODUCTION

FLOW

IS THE

RHYTHM

OF THE

RHYMES,

AND EVERY

WORD.

EVERY

SYLLABLE,

AFFECTS IT.

Practice makes perfect? Nah. Practice makes greatness.

If you know anything about me, you know that I am a basketball fangirl. WNBA, NBA, NCAA, all of it. I would watch games every single day if I could. But I'm never able to watch the most important part of the game because they don't air it.

The most important part of the game is practice.

WNBA great Candace Parker is known to practice two to three times per day. Per. Day. LeBron James, too. Steph Curry shoots five hundred shots daily. When Kobe Bryant was still in high school, he practiced four hours daily . . . before and after school.

That's dedication right there.

People often say that practice makes perfect, but honestly that phrase should be retired. Nobody is perfect. (Nope, not even you. Sorry.) Even those basketball players I just mentioned have their flaws. But every single one of them is great.

Practice doesn't make perfect. Nah. Practice makes greatness.

Unfortunately, I can't shoot a three-pointer or pull off a crossover. Writing is where it's at for me. So why not approach my craft the same way LeBron approaches his? That means making practice the most important part of writing. How do you practice for writing? The answer is simple, I swear.

You write.

You write small projects; you write big ones. You write fanfiction, you write short stories, you write a paragraph, you write a sentence. You write for yourself.

You write.

You write.

You write.

While the goal of this journal is to help you discover and develop a writing project, aka the big game, you still gotta practice for it. I suggest keeping a journal. Nothing fancy, but if you want it to be fancy, that's fine, too. Whatever works for you. You just need to write. Ten, fifteen, or even thirty minutes every day would be a great start. And just like Curry getting those five hundred shots up daily, you'll find yourself getting better and better. You'll find your voice getting stronger. Even better, you'll start to see yourself as a writer.

Because guess what? If you write, you're a writer.

Yeah, you. You're a writer. In fact, for the rest of the journal, I'm going to refer to you as Writer with a capital *W* because you're legit.

Now that we've gotten that established, let's get this thing started.

Q: Where Do Stories Come From?
A: When a Writer and an Idea Fall in Love . . .

I think the question I am asked the most is where do I get my ideas from. I wish I could say that story ideas just fall from the sky and in seconds I have an entire book figured out. (Ha! If only.)

For me and for most writers, story ideas usually come from a couple of sources: an idea, an emotion, or an observation. Usually we're desperate to express and explore that idea, emotion, or observation because it nags at us so much; it takes up space in our thoughts, our imaginations.

Now, the difference between an aspiring writer and a writer is that a writer makes the choice to express or explore. An aspiring writer just thinks about those ideas and lets them sit in their head for ages.

If this feels like an attack on you, Writer, I'm sorry. Now go write ☺.

But seriously, we all have ideas that we think would make a good story, but we ultimately let fear get in the way. We're scared that we're not good enough to write the story, we're scared of what people will think. Blah, blah, blah. But at some point, Writer, we have to let our desire to tell the story outweigh our fear.

Look, I get it. Believe me, I do. I was afraid to write both *The Hate U Give* and *On the Come Up*. I first got the idea for *THUG* while in college. I felt so much anger, frustration, and pain when it came to police brutality and felt writing was the best way to express myself.

However, I was afraid of what people would think. I was even more afraid with *On the Come Up* because so much of it is my personal story. Putting it in the world would be like exposing a new part of myself. Both books were born from a desire to speak and express myself, but it was terrifying.

Yet the desire to express those ideas, emotions, and observations were so strong that I had to write. I had to tell these stories; I had to tell *my* story.

Thing is, our stories don't have to represent exactly who we are. But almost always, they will be about something that's meaningful to us. It's your passion and truth-telling that make your voice worth hearing.

So ask yourself: What are some experiences I've had or heard of, things I've seen or done that I want to share? Return to these pages to add to your list whenever you think of something. If this were basketball practice, consider this your ball rack.

All right. So you have an idea or ideas that have been in your head for a while, and you want to write, but there's a big question that's been keeping you from doing so:

WHAT IF MY IDEA ISN'T GOOD ENOUGH?

I can only imagine how many potential books have never been born simply because the writer was afraid their idea wasn't good enough. It's one of the biggest fears a writer can have.

What makes a story "good enough" though? To answer that, we have to ask ourselves what makes a story interesting. Think about people you know who tell good stories. No, they don't have to be writers. It could be that uncle who keeps everyone laughing with tales of his shenanigans or the hairstylist who knows everything about everyone. When they tell stories, they do it in a way that keeps people listening. The best storytellers don't just list what happened; listeners won't stay interested then. The best storytellers get their listeners invested in the outcome to the point that they feel what the person is going through in the story.

How do good storytellers make you feel what the character feels? By keeping the events of the story attached to the emotions and desires of the characters. What happened doesn't matter without the character's feelings about it. When they don't just tell what happened but make it clear why it mattered and how they felt about it, then we feel like we've had that experience too.

In *The Hate U Give,* sure, I could have had Starr witness the killing of a boy in the neighborhood she wasn't close to. It would have been a way different story though, and probably less emotional. I could have made Hailey just some girl at Starr's school. But since Hailey was supposed to be Starr's friend, the things she did and said had an extra sting—for Starr and for the reader. I've had plenty of readers tell me they cried over Khalil's death—Starr's attachment to him made them attached to him as well. And I have a whole lot of readers say they want to knock some sense into Hailey; they felt what Starr felt.

That's the thing though: People like stories that make us think and feel in a new way or that express something we have felt in our lives too. The art of storytelling is in making the listener or reader feel the emotions, dilemmas, and consequences by bringing them on a journey without telling them how to feel. If you do it right, Writer, the feelings will come naturally.

Try this: Think of a story someone told you: not a book but an oral story someone told you about an experience they had or witnessed. If you remember the story, it must have been pretty good, right? Now ask yourself, Why did I keep listening? What was the point of the story? How did it feel to hear it?

Write down the story's basic action in three or four sentences, without emotion. Then write down all the thoughts, emotions, and ideas it brought up as it was told. Did the teller have to name these emotions, or did you feel them automatically because you knew why the events mattered to the person? When you write, keep in mind this connection between the facts and why they matter.

_____

_____

_____

_____

_____

_____

_____

_____

_____

_____

_____

_____

_____

_____

nothing's

BEEN *the* SAME

SINCE

NAS

TOLD ME

the

WORLD

was mine.

PART 1

CHOOSING A
STORY IDEA

IT'S
ONE THING
TO WANNA DO
SOMETHING.

IT'S ANOTHER
TO THINK IT'S
POSSIBLE.

Brainstorming

We've talked about ideas, where they come from, how fear can get in the way, all of that. But hey, you still may be struggling to choose an idea for your story. Well, this section is here to help you explore it.

For the timed exercises, you want to get every possible idea down on paper, no matter how ridiculous or unclear it may seem at first. I repeat: no matter how ridiculous or unclear it may seem. Don't worry about that now, Writer. So when you set a timer, don't stop writing until the timer goes off. Period.

What is something so interesting or important to you that you could write a whole lot about it without getting bored? There are different ways to come to a story idea. Here are some ways to try.

1. Start with a theme or subject.
What are your obsessions? What are you curious about? What are you passionate about?

Set a timer for one minute and write down everything you have strong feelings about. Nothing is too big or too small, too general or too specific. When you get to the story level, you'll find a way to narrow it down or expand it if you need to.

Once the timer has gone off, pick three things from

the list you just made. Spend one minute on each item and brainstorm or freewrite about it. You can do a word association or list every action and image that comes to mind related to it. Just see where it takes you. You are looking for story seeds. Remember, write everything that comes to mind, and don't stop writing until the timer goes off. Don't. Stop. Writing. Until. The. Timer. Goes. Off. Now go.

_____

_____

_____

_____

_____

_____

_____

_____

_____

_____

_____

_____

_____

_____

_____

_____

_____

_____

ONE SONG.

IS SOMETIMES

ALL IT TAKES.

I'VE GOT

ONE SONG.

2. Start with a character.

Is there a person, a community, or a way of being in the world that you want to explore?

Set a timer for two minutes and write down names of individuals, communities, or character types. For each name or type, write down three adjectives or character traits to describe them.

_____

_____

_____

_____

_____

_____

_____

_____

_____

_____

_____

_____

_____

_____

_____

_____

_____

_____

Once the timer has gone off, pick your top two from that list. Now set the timer for three minutes and write a paragraph or two describing this person or community and why they matter to you. What do you want to hear them say in a story? After you've sketched one, set the timer for another three minutes and sketch the other.

_____

_____

_____

_____

_____

_____

_____

_____

_____

_____

_____

_____

_____

_____

_____

_____

_____

_____

_____

_____

3. Start with a plot idea.

Do you already have a "what-if" scenario you want to explore? The "what-if" is the premise of a story.

For *On the Come Up*, you could say, "What if a young, aspiring rapper makes a song that goes viral for all the wrong reasons? What if her family is struggling and she's so desperate to make it that she's willing to go to any lengths? How would she deal with all of the drama that follows?"

Write your "what-if" question. It may take several tries. Keep at it until you have a question that leads to a need for actions and decisions on the part of the protagonist.

_____

_____

_____

_____

_____

_____

_____

_____

_____

_____

_____

_____

_____

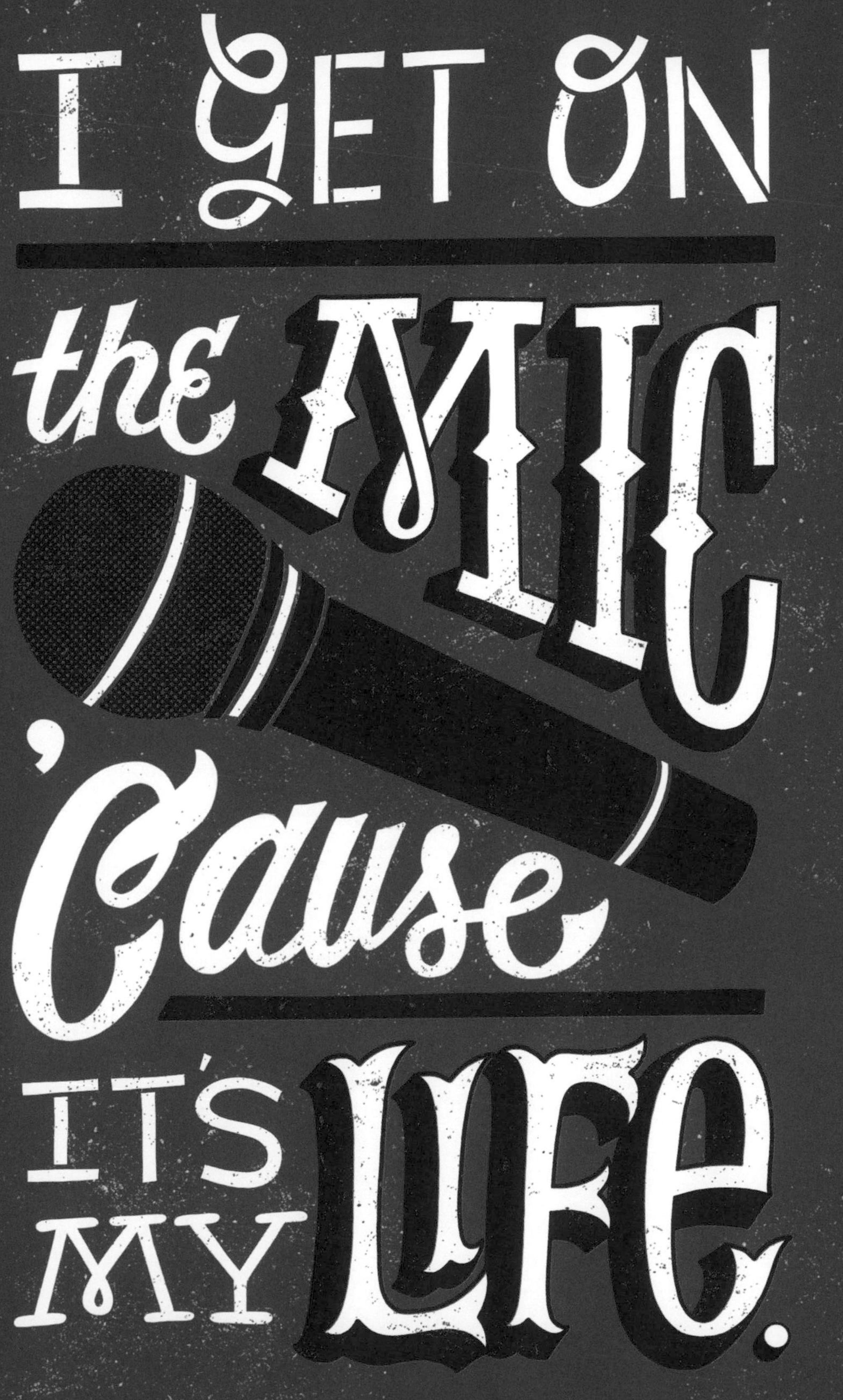
I GET ON
the MIC
'Cause
IT'S MY LIFE.

From Question to Scenario

Once you have a good "what-if" question, set a timer for six minutes and answer the question as fully as you can. You can use an action-reaction pattern to develop a sequence of events. To make this a really useful exercise, connect each action and reaction with "so" or "but." You are building up not only what happens but why.

For example, for *On the Come Up,* the answer to the "what-if" question would go like this:

> *She would be frustrated and hurt that people took her song the wrong way and that they're making assumptions about her. But it would also help her make a name for herself. So since her family's situation is bad, she would feel like she has to become what people think she is in order to make it. So she might go along with it at first . . .*

Each action and reaction can grow into a scene, a chapter, or a part of your story.

Your answer to the "what-if" question is the main plot of your story. You will come back to it again and again.

Developing Your Idea

Okay, Writer. Look back at what you wrote in the three brainstorming sections. If you really wrote everything that came to mind (and I hope you did), some ideas will attract you more than others. If you know which idea you want to pursue, circle it. If you're still not sure, that's okay. Pick your top three ideas, drawing from any of the three sections.

Take the next few pages to write down every thought you have about these ideas, one idea at a time. You can freewrite, journal, create a mind map, or just make lists. Phrases, feelings, actions, and conflicts are good, but any idea can be a key to some crucial piece of your story. Write it all down.

_____

_____

_____

_____

_____

_____

_____

THAT'S WHY
PEOPLE ARE
SPEAKING
OUT, HUH?
BECAUSE
IT WON'T
CHANGE IF
WE DON'T SAY
SOMETHING.

Now, which idea is pulling you the most? Which one would you think about all the time? Which one is most urgent for you to tell?

_____

_____

_____

_____

_____

_____

_____

_____

_____

_____

_____

_____

_____

_____

_____

_____

Motivation

Now write down *why* you want to tell this story. When your motivation gets low (and believe me, it will. It happens to all of us), come back to this purpose page to remind yourself why you're writing.

_____

_____

_____

_____

_____

_____

_____

_____

_____

_____

_____

_____

_____

_____

_____

_____

PART 2

GET TO KNOW YOUR CHARACTERS

She spits like an OLD SOUL, as if she's lived a couple of LIFETIMES and didn't like EITHER one of them.

Characters

Who is your protagonist? What does your protagonist want? What stands in their way? How do they change by the end of the story? These are the basic questions that will drive your story. But you also need a deep understanding of who your character is and how their personality traits lead to action and struggle that make sense in your story. This is one of the most vital parts of developing a story. Always connect the action to your character's main conflict and perspective. The reader cares only because the character cares.

MAIN CHARACTER SURVEY

It's time to get to know your main character(s). These are things that may never appear in your story, but you will write a better story because you know your character so well. For instance, in *The Hate U Give,* I knew that Starr was a sneakerhead. In the story, we see her love for sneakers sprinkled throughout. But it also affected the plot: Early on, when she sees Khalil at the party, she immediately recognizes that he's wearing expensive sneakers that he shouldn't be able to afford, leading her to believe he's making money by selling drugs.

So, see, when you know things about your character, you can use them in the plot.

And when you know their background, you can make them sound real.

Ask yourself questions about your characters to flesh them out. When's your character's birthday? What's their zodiac sign? How does that affect their personality if you believe in that kind of stuff? What's their favorite music genre? What's their Hogwarts House? Team Edward or Team Jacob? If they had a million dollars, what's the first thing they would do with it? These may seem like silly questions, but they can reveal a lot about your character(s). Here are some questions you can use to get started, but you can totally come up with more.

1. What are four main character traits? Try coming up with two positive traits and two negative traits. Then list how these traits affect the character's interactions with other people and his environment. When do his positive traits become a problem? When do his negative traits work for him?

_____

_____

_____

_____

_____

_____

_____

2. What does their bedroom look like? What things will you find in there?

_____

_____

_____

_____

_____

_____

_____

_____

3. If this character got a week to do anything they wanted, how would they spend it?

_____

_____

_____

_____

_____

_____

_____

_____

_____

_____

_____

4. What is this character's favorite place to hang out? Why?

_____

_____

_____

_____

_____

_____

_____

_____

5. What's this character's favorite food? Is there a memory attached to it?

_____

_____

_____

_____

_____

_____

_____

_____

_____

_____

_____

6. How is this character different at home, at school, at work, et cetera?

_____

_____

_____

_____

_____

_____

_____

_____

_____

_____

_____

_____

_____

_____

_____

_____

_____

_____

_____

_____

7. Who is this character's favorite person at the beginning of the story? Why? Does that person deserve this character's love and loyalty?

_____

_____

_____

_____

_____

_____

_____

_____

_____

_____

_____

_____

_____

_____

_____

_____

_____

_____

_____

_____

_____

8. Name a topic this character knows everything about. How did he first get interested in this topic? Is their knowledge and ability in this area valued by those around them?

_____

_____

_____

_____

_____

_____

_____

_____

_____

_____

_____

_____

_____

_____

_____

_____

_____

_____

_____

9. If this character likes to read, what is their favorite book?
Who introduced it to them? Or do they hate reading?

_____

_____

_____

_____

_____

_____

_____

_____

_____

_____

_____

_____

_____

_____

_____

_____

_____

_____

_____

_____

10. Describe the character's family dynamics. How does each person in the house feel about the others? How do they treat each other?

_____

_____

_____

_____

_____

_____

_____

_____

_____

_____

_____

_____

_____

_____

_____

_____

_____

_____

_____

_____

11. What does this character sound like? Write some words and phrases they use a lot and how they say them. Hear them in your mind and write down what they sound like. Try writing a conversation or a journal entry in their voice. Make a playlist of the character's favorite songs. What lyrics does the character especially relate to?*

_____

_____

_____

_____

_____

_____

_____

_____

_____

_____

_____

_____

_____

_____

_____

_____

_____

_____

*You can check out my writing playlists for The Hate U Give and On the Come Up on Spotify.

IT SEEMS KINDA MYTHICAL, THAT I'D BE CALLED A MIRACLE

Secondary Characters

You should know something about every single character in your story. Yep, every single one. Just like random people you pass in the real world, every character in your created world has their own story, their own desires, struggles, and conflicts. You should especially know your secondary characters. Doing so will help you create scenes that feel real, with emotional depth. More importantly, it will help you create three-dimensional characters; your MC shouldn't be forced to interact with cardboard cutouts.

Try this shorter character survey to get to know secondary characters that will play a role in your protagonist's story. Don't forget about the antagonist, if you have one!

CHARACTER 1

1. Four main character traits:

_____

_____

_____

_____

_____

_____

_____

_____

2. A few objects in their bedroom:

_____

_____

_____

_____

3. Favorite book:

_____

_____

_____

_____

_____

_____

4. Obsession:

_____

_____

_____

_____

_____

5. Family dynamics:

_____

_____

_____

_____

_____

_____

_____

_____

_____

6. Speech patterns:

_____

_____

_____

_____

_____

_____

7. How does this character affect the main character's story? Is their story a subplot? Does it complicate or help solve the main plot?

_____

_____

_____

_____

_____

_____

_____

_____

_____

_____

_____

_____

_____

_____

_____

_____

_____

_____

_____

CHARACTER 2

1. Four main character traits:

_____

_____

_____

_____

_____

_____

_____

2. A few objects in their bedroom:

_____

_____

_____

_____

_____

3. Favorite book:

_____

_____

_____

_____

_____

_____

4. Obsession:

_____

_____

_____

_____

_____

5. Family dynamics:

_____

_____

_____

_____

_____

_____

_____

_____

_____

6. Speech patterns:

_____

_____

_____

_____

_____

_____

7. How does this character affect the main character's story? Is their story a subplot? Does it complicate or help solve the main plot?

_____

_____

_____

_____

_____

_____

_____

_____

_____

_____

_____

_____

_____

_____

_____

_____

_____

_____

_____

_____

_____

CHARACTER 3

1. Four main character traits:

_____

_____

_____

_____

_____

_____

_____

_____

2. A few objects in their bedroom:

_____

_____

_____

_____

_____

3. Favorite book:

_____

_____

_____

_____

_____

_____

4. Obsession:

_____

_____

_____

_____

_____

5. Family dynamics:

_____

_____

_____

_____

_____

_____

_____

_____

_____

6. Speech patterns:

_____

_____

_____

_____

_____

_____

7. How does this character affect the main character's story? Is their story a subplot? Does it complicate or help solve the main plot?

_____

_____

_____

_____

_____

_____

_____

_____

_____

_____

_____

_____

_____

_____

_____

_____

_____

_____

_____

CHARACTER 4

1. Four main character traits:

_____

_____

_____

_____

_____

_____

_____

_____

2. A few objects in their bedroom:

_____

_____

_____

_____

_____

3. Favorite book:

_____

_____

_____

_____

_____

_____

4. Obsession:

_____

_____

_____

_____

_____

5. Family dynamics:

_____

_____

_____

_____

_____

_____

_____

_____

_____

_____

6. Speech patterns:

_____

_____

_____

_____

_____

_____

7. How does this character affect the main character's story? Is their story a subplot? Does it complicate or help solve the main plot?

_____

_____

_____

_____

_____

_____

_____

_____

_____

_____

_____

_____

_____

_____

_____

_____

_____

_____

_____

CHARACTER 5

1. Four main character traits:

_____

_____

_____

_____

_____

_____

_____

2. A few objects in their bedroom:

_____

_____

_____

_____

3. Favorite book:

_____

_____

_____

_____

_____

_____

4. Obsession:

_____

_____

_____

_____

_____

5. Family dynamics:

_____

_____

_____

_____

_____

_____

_____

_____

_____

6. Speech patterns:

_____

_____

_____

_____

_____

_____

7. How does this character affect the main character's story? Is their story a subplot? Does it complicate or help solve the main plot?

_____

_____

_____

_____

_____

_____

_____

_____

_____

_____

_____

_____

_____

_____

_____

_____

_____

_____

_____

_____

ADDITIONAL NOTES

I Realize **BEING REAL AIN'T GOT ANYTHING** TO DO WITH WHERE *You Live.*

Setting

When your reader opens your book, Writer, they are entering a world, whether it's realistic or fantasy, whether it's based on an actual place or completely fictional. You need to know what that world looks and feels like so you can make your reader feel and see it too.

When I wrote *The Hate U Give*, I had to show how Starr is between two different worlds and how those worlds shape who she is and also shape her conflict. I had to show how pressure came from different places in those worlds. Use the following questions to think about how setting shapes your characters and your story, just like in real life our environment shapes who we are and what we do.

1. How do you want this world to be unique? How do you want it to stand out?

_____

_____

_____

_____

_____

2. How does your character feel about the setting?

_____

_____

_____

_____

_____

_____

_____

_____

_____

3. How does the setting affect the characters? Does it add pressure? Reflect characters' feelings and moods? Intensify conflict?

_____

_____

_____

_____

_____

_____

_____

_____

_____

_____

_____

Draw a map of the area where the main action occurs. It doesn't have to be artistic. Believe me, the map I created of Garden Heights was made up of lines and boxes; I cannot draw for the life of me. You're only doing this to get a lay of the land so you can see your characters moving through the world in your mind. Label the important places.

Obstacles, Struggles, and Conflict

Okay, so you know your characters. You know the setting. Now you should be able to create some conflicts that come naturally from the personalities you have and the setting they are in. We finish a book not just to see *what* happens at the end but *how* it happens. The character's journey from beginning to end is what we're after. The character should have a bunch of obstacles to overcome, or learn to deal with, on their way. Here is where you develop some of those obstacles.

1. What is the protagonist's main desire in the story, and what is the major thing that keeps them from getting it? (The obstacle can be a person, thing, or idea. Maybe it's a fear or a personality flaw in the character.)

_____

_____

_____

_____

_____

_____

_____

2. Reread all your character sketches and your description of your setting. Set the timer for three minutes and write down every possible conflict or problem that could happen with these characters in this setting. List as many as you can.

_____

_____

_____

_____

_____

_____

_____

_____

_____

_____

_____

_____

_____

_____

_____

_____

_____

_____

_____

_____

_____

3. Go through the list you just created and highlight the problems you would like to see appear in your story. Now copy them below, leaving space between each one. Each of these problems is an action. Now list the reaction for each one. What happens because of this problem or action? Eventually, the entire plot will be connected as a series of problem-solution or action-reaction events. This is similar to the "what-if" scenario, but here you are getting more specific.

_____

_____

_____

_____

_____

_____

_____

_____

_____

_____

_____

_____

_____

_____

_____

PART 3

WRITING YOUR "ZERO DRAFT"

No fallacies,
I spit maladies,
causin' fatalities,
And do it casually,
damaging rappers
without bandaging.
Imagining managing
my own label,
my own salary.
And actually,
factually,
there's no MC
that's as bad as me.

It surprises people when I tell them that I never write a first draft first. I always start with a zero draft. What's a zero draft, you ask? It's a way for me to get to know my characters. No one else ever reads it, so I don't worry about it making sense. It can be random scenes, such as my characters with their family or them at their job or their school. It allows me to understand them, their motivations, their voices, their relationships, et cetera, at a deeper level. Again, the zero draft doesn't have to make sense or even follow a structure. It's a place to explore. Feel free to try things out. For instance, you can see which feels best for the story, first or third person, by writing in both. If something doesn't work, it's okay. Try something new or change things up.

In this section, try out some scenes. When you feel stuck, check out the craft tips and exercises.

Craft Tip: Description

When you open up a book and see long paragraphs of description, how does it feel? For me personally, I get bored easily. Too much description can make me put the book down. So, Writer, be selective when describing. Trust your reader more. You don't have to describe every single detail for them to get the idea. Mostly, you want to "show" through action and dialogue that make the reader feel what you mean instead of telling them the actions and feelings. That is the difference between a strong story and a summary.

When you have to describe things in the character's world, make sure you describe it from the character's perspective. Use the character's voice and focus on what the character would notice. That way, description is also character-building and world-building.

Exercise: Your character comes home with a friend who has never been to her house before. What does the character notice now that she never usually notices? Write this in a short scene, in your character's voice.

I've Taught
MYSELF
TO SPEAK WITH TWO
Different
VOICES

Craft Tip: Dialogue

Every single person in your life sounds different in some way. Honestly, they do. They may use certain words more than others or cut off certain words. They may have accents or different speech patterns. Really think about your friends, your family, your teachers. What makes each person's voice unique? Some things we can only hear, but some aspects of voice we can capture on paper.

An example of this is with the characters of Sonny and Malik in *On the Come Up*.

They're both the main character Bri's best friends, and they're both sixteen-year-old boys from the same neighborhood, yet they speak differently. Sonny is more direct, so his sentences are shorter. Malik can ramble at times, especially when he's nervous. Sonny will reference pop culture, while Malik will reference nerd culture. Simple things like that help them sound different.

Another example is from *The Hate U Give*. Starr's father, Maverick, and her uncle, Carlos, sound completely different from each other. They too are around the same age and are from the same neighborhood, yet they could say the same idea in totally different ways. Maverick uses African American Vernacular at times, and Carlos doesn't. That, too, adds to their personalities and backgrounds.

If you make your characters talk with a unique voice, readers should be able to follow their conversations with only a few dialogue tags ("he said"/ "she said").

Exercise: Practice writing a conversation between your main character and someone of a different age or background, without writing dialogue tags. See if a reader would be able to follow who is talking when. (Be warned: This is hard to do! It's just practice!)

_____

_____

_____

_____

_____

_____

_____

_____

_____

_____

_____

_____

_____

_____

_____

Craft Tip: Scenes

What makes a good scene? Every good scene has an arc of its own and some action that changes things. The main character goes in wanting or expecting something. Do they get it? Things are different at the end of the scene, even if only in their head. How do they feel about how things went? The next action happens because of what happened here. Based on this outcome, what is their next move? Keep this arc in mind for every scene.

_____

_____

_____

_____

_____

_____

_____

_____

_____

_____

_____

_____

_____

YOU

CAN'T

Stop Me,

NOPE,

NOPE.

PEOPLE
don't know the
WHOLE
STORY.

Craft Tip: Subplots

Look at what you have so far and see what can be developed into subplots, if given a little more attention. Try writing a scene that brings a subplot closer to center stage. Always keep in touch with why it matters to the main character and their main conflict or desire.

_____

_____

_____

_____

_____

_____

_____

_____

_____

_____

_____

_____

_____

Now pick five problems—maybe the biggest ones—and sketch the scenes in which these problems happen. Focus on action and reaction and include how the characters feel about everything. What do they go into the scene wanting? What changes during the scene? By the end of the scene, what have they decided to do next?

Those Words Feel as Good as Any Hug I've Ever Gotten.

I'M SOMEBODY'S HOPE. AND I'M SOMEBODY'S MIRROR.

That
FLOW
THOUGH!

_____

_____

_____

_____

_____

_____

_____

_____

_____

_____

_____

_____

_____

_____

_____

Have you finished your zero draft? Use a blank notebook if you need more space. Once you've finished your zero draft, it's time to celebrate! It may look messy. That's okay! This is the raw material that will become your story. Some writers call it compost. Some call it cake batter. I personally call it my precious. Whatever you want to call it, it's something to work with. Before you go on—before you even read what you wrote—celebrate that you've created something! You're a writer, Writer!

STORY
STRUCTURE AND
OUTLINING

WHAT'S THE POINT OF HAVING A VOICE

IF YOU'RE GONNA BE SILENT IN THOSE MOMENTS YOU SHOULDN'T BE?

All right, now it's time to work on that first draft. Some writers choose to write their first draft without an outline. For me, making a basic outline means less work in revision. This section will help you organize and develop your ideas to get you ready to write your first draft.

Narrative Arc

Most novels have an overall shape that can be broken down to look sort of like the three acts of a play.

Act One is exposition. This is where readers get to know who the character is before the change happens and what their normal world is like. By the end of act one, some new thing will be introduced that has the potential to change their life as they know it. Readers will understand the importance of the change based on what we've learned about the protagonist's life so far.

Act Two is where the plot gets complicated. The main character pursues their desire while obstacle after obstacle comes at them to prevent them from getting it. The obstacles keep getting bigger until the biggest obstacle forces the main character to give it their all.

In **Act Three**, you have a climax scene where the main character makes a major decision and faces their biggest obstacle. Unless you're writing a tragedy, your main character will finally succeed, and often the success will feel different than they thought it would. The action will be resolved quickly, and a final scene will leave the reader with an image or idea that will stay with them long after they've closed the book.

Got it? Good. Now let's sketch out the action of your story in three acts.

ACT ONE

Sketch an opening that will show who your character is. Where are they? Who else is there? What is your main character doing? What are they wearing? What are they talking about? What do they expect will happen next? What big change comes along to launch them on their mission?

_____

_____

_____

_____

_____

_____

_____

_____

_____

ACT TWO

What is their first plan to deal with the problem that just showed up? Why doesn't that work? How do they try to fix the next complication, and how does that backfire? Keep spiraling until they are backed into a corner. You may feel bad for putting them through all of this, but hey, it's a story. Keep going.

_____

_____

_____

_____

_____

_____

_____

_____

_____

_____

_____

_____

_____

_____

_____

_____

_____

_____

ACT THREE

It's now or never. This is the final test. What does it take for them to face it, and how do you show it? How are they different now compared to the beginning because of all they've gone through? How do you show the change to the reader? How do you want the reader to feel at the end?

_____

_____

_____

_____

_____

_____

_____

_____

_____

_____

_____

_____

_____

_____

_____

_____

_____

ROYALTY in my BLOOD DIDN'T Choose IT

Calendar or Timeline

Now you know the order of the major events. To pace the story and to plan the plot, it helps to make a calendar or timeline so you know when each event happens and how long the story takes from beginning to end. The calendar will also help with setting. It will determine what time of year it is and what seasons and holidays might be in the background, setting the mood—knowing your setting will help with this, too. (Winter in Hawaii is totally different from winter in Colorado.) This allows you to ground the action in the world of the story. I can't stress enough how important this is in creating your world. The sooner you do it, the better.

Use these pages to sketch a calendar or timeline. Remember that events don't have to be written in chronological order. Some events may be written as flashbacks, and you may choose to skip around in time. This calendar is for you to keep the story clear in your mind.

MONTH: _____

YEAR: _____

			1	2	3	4
5	6	7	8	9	10	11
12	13	14	15	16	17	18
19	20	21	22	23	24	25
26	27	28	29	30	31	

MONTH: _____

YEAR: _____

	1	2	3	4	5	6
7	8	9	10	11	12	13
14	15	16	17	18	19	20
21	22	23	24	25	26	27
28	29	30	31			

MONTH: _____

YEAR: _____

1	2	3	4	5	6	7
8	9	10	11	12	13	14
15	16	17	18	19	20	21
22	23	24	25	26	27	28
29	30	31				

God Gave You a Brain.

YOU DON'T NEED THEIRS.

PART 5

GETTING FEEDBACK

When you've finished your first draft, you might decide it's ready to share for feedback. Or you might already know what you need to work on in your next draft. In that case, you might try a rewrite and get it closer to your vision before you share it. So this section and the next section can be used whenever you are ready. But you will need to do both of these steps, probably several times, before your story will be ready to share with the world. Trust me: Every book you've ever read has been through multiple drafts and revisions. Yes, even this journal you're reading at this very moment. Also keep in mind that first drafts are meant to be awful. So, don't fret. Just revise.

Before You Get Feedback

1. After yourself, who are you writing for? Is there one person who, if they get it, no one else matters? See if this person is willing to read your book. If they're not a reader, see if they'll listen to you read your book to them. Watching them react will give you a lot of information. What parts have them quietly listening? (Interested.) What parts have them picking up their phone to scroll or remembering something else they need to be doing? (Bored.) When

do they stop you to ask clarifying questions? (Confused.) I always read my books aloud to my mom, and believe me, her reactions tell me a whole lot.

_____

_____

_____

_____

_____

_____

_____

_____

_____

_____

_____

_____

_____

_____

_____

_____

_____

_____

_____

2. Only you know why you wrote this story. You get the final decisions about what stays and what goes. Before you hand over your manuscript for someone else to read, remind yourself of why you wrote it, and jot down what elements you are not willing to change. (You are allowed to change your mind later if you're convinced that your reasons for including it are not coming across to the reader. For now, for yourself, list the things you aren't open to changing.)

_____

_____

_____

_____

_____

_____

_____

_____

_____

_____

_____

_____

_____

_____

_____

_____

Finding a Trusted Reader

You are looking for someone who can give you kind, honest feedback. Do some research about places in your area, like public libraries and community centers, that might have youth writing groups, a writer in residence, or other resources. Do you already have a mentor who might be able to read your work? A teacher? List every possible resource that might be a starting point for finding someone.

_____

_____

_____

_____

_____

_____

_____

_____

_____

_____

_____

_____

_____

_____

What Do You Need to Know?

I can't say this enough: Every draft needs some work. Every. Draft. It might feel nice if someone reads your writing and says, "I love it!" That's encouraging, but it won't help you improve. You need to know what parts work and why, and what parts don't work and why not. Help your reader to help you by giving them specific questions to answer about your story.

Brainstorm some questions to give your reader. Write down as many as you like on the next page, but choose less than ten questions to give each reader. You don't want to overwhelm them. It can be helpful to give them a printed copy of your story so they can write on the pages.

Here are some possible questions to get you started. Let them know you will only improve if they are honest with you, but you will only have the courage to improve if they are kind about it. Give them your questions with a copy of the story so they can mark as they read.

1. What did you like best about the story?
2. What confused you?
3. Did you like the main character? Why or why not?
4. Please mark the places where you got bored.

5. Please mark the places where you got confused.

6. Please mark the parts you could relate to.

7. Please mark the parts you thought were not realistic.

_____

_____

_____

_____

_____

_____

_____

_____

_____

_____

_____

_____

_____

_____

_____

_____

_____

_____

_____

_____

_____

After Getting Feedback

Once your reader gives you feedback, sit with it for a while before doing anything about it. Some feedback may sting, especially if the things you thought were working aren't working for this reader. It's totally okay to get a second opinion. And a third. Even a fourth. Wait a while before making changes. Their advice might make more sense to you after you let it marinate a bit. But in the end, know that you control the story and changes are ultimately up to you.

When you're ready to decide what feedback to use and what to reject, go back to your list of nonnegotiables. Everything that's not on your list is up for grabs. If it won't mess with your vision, and your message can still get through, play with the suggestions and see where they lead.

PART 6

REWRITING AND REVISING

THIS WILL CHANGE your LIFE WITH A FEW LINES.

You wrote your first draft. Congrats! You may have gotten some feedback, and even if the feedback hurts, celebrate yourself regardless—you wrote something, Writer. Now it's time to shape up your story by writing another draft.

Yeah, another draft. You are not done yet. Sorry, Writer.

First things first—if you haven't already, take a break! Please, please take a break. You need a vacation from the story before you can come back to it with fresh eyes. You want to be able to read it like it's your first time so you can really recognize the good stuff from the not so good. Take a few days, a week, or even a month away. Your story will be better for it.

Next, plan a day to reread the entire draft in one sitting. You want to see everything you have and get a bird's-eye view of what's there.

Then ask yourself some big-picture questions.

1. Did you do what you set out to do? Did you come to a new understanding or express the idea or perspective you wanted to express?

_____

_____

_____

_____

_____

_____

_____

_____

_____

_____

_____

_____

_____

_____

_____

_____

_____

_____

_____

_____

_____

2. What do you want to say louder in your next draft? What do you want to show more of?

_____

_____

_____

_____

_____

_____

_____

_____

_____

_____

_____

_____

_____

_____

_____

_____

_____

_____

_____

_____

_____

_____

_____

3. What distractions are in your story that don't need to be there? If they aren't really a part of your story, you should consider cutting them out. Save them for later. They might be the seeds for your next story!

_____

_____

_____

_____

_____

_____

_____

_____

_____

_____

_____

_____

_____

_____

_____

_____

_____

_____

_____

Rewriting versus Revising

Rewriting is taking your material and molding it into a new shape. You may start with what you have and work from it, or you may put it aside and start all over again, trusting that your mind will call up the important parts and put them down more precisely.

Revising is taking your finished piece and polishing it until it shines. You do this when your draft is telling the story you want it to tell in the way you want to tell it and you just need to make sure every sentence, paragraph, and scene is in the best shape you can manage.

You may need to do ten rewrites and one revision, or one major rewrite and five revisions. It will take a lot of work and a lot of time. You have everything you need to finish your story. Keep going, Writer. You have stories to tell.

I'LL NEVER
GIVE UP.
I'LL NEVER
BE QUIET.
I promise.

Resources

Writing Fiction: A Guide to Narrative Craft, Tenth Edition by Janet Burroway (University of Chicago Press, 2019)

Writing Fiction: A Hands-On Guide for Teens by Heather Wright (iUniverse, 2010)

National Novel Writing Month Young Writers Program
www.ywp.nanowrimo.org

Wattpad
www.wattpad.com

The Writers' Helpers
www.thewritershelpers.tumblr.com

Teen Ink
www.teenink.com

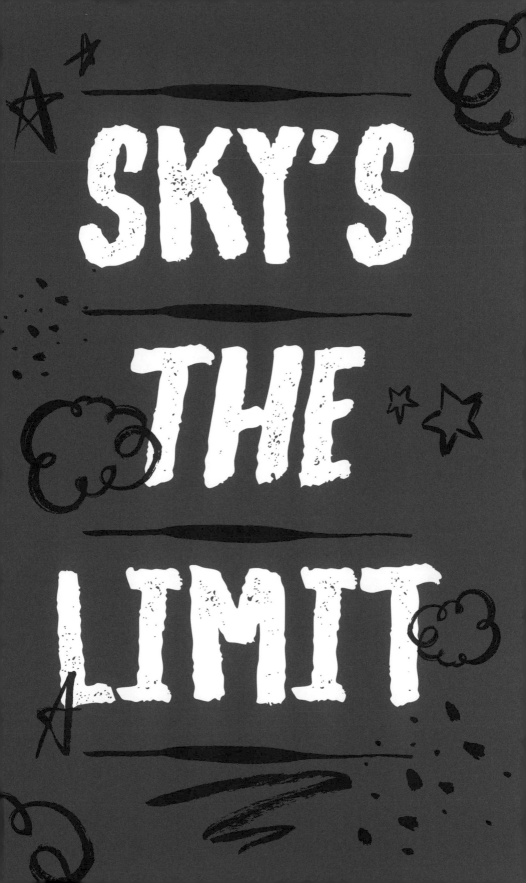

The author wishes to thank Autumn Allen
for her help in creating this journal.

First published in Great Britain 2020 by Walker Books Ltd
87 Vauxhall Walk, London, SE11 5HJ

2 4 6 8 10 9 7 5 3 1

This book has been typeset in Latienne

Printed and bound in Italy

British Library Cataloguing in Publication Data:
a catalogue record for this book is available from the British Library

ISBN 978-1-4063-9710-9

www.walker.co.uk